STAR PILOT

P9-CFU-444

Written by Laura Buller and Tori Kosara

Penguin
Random
House

Senior Editor Tori Kosara
Project Editor Lisa Stock
Editor Anant Sagar
Art Editor Karan Chaudhary
DTP Designer Umesh Singh Rawat
Pre-production Producer Siu Yin Chan
Pre-production Manager Sunil Sharma
Senior Producer Alex Bell
Managing Editors Sadie Smith, Chitra Subramanyam
Managing Art Editors Neha Ahuja, Ron Stobbart
Publisher Julie Ferris
Art Director Lisa Lanzarini
Publishing Director Simon Beecroft

Designed for DK by Mark Richards

For Lucasfilm
Executive Editor Jonathan W. Rinzler
Art Director Troy Alders
Story Group Rayne Roberts, Pablo Hidalgo, Leland Chee

Reading Consultant Linda B. Gambrell

First American Edition, 2015
Published in the United States by DK Publishing
345 Hudson Street, New York 10014

Copyright © 2015 Dorling Kindersley Limited
A Penguin Random House Company

15 16 17 18 19 10 9 8 7 6 5 4 3 2 1
001-276427-Sep/15

© & TM 2015 LUCASFILM LTD.

A catalog record for this book is available from the Library of Congress.

ISBN: 978-1-4654-3387-9 (Hardcover)
ISBN: 978-1-4654-3388-6 (Paperback)

DK books are available at special discounts when purchased in bulk for sales
promotions, premiums, fund-raising, or educational use. For details, contact:
DK Publishing Special Markets, 345 Hudson Street, New York, New York 10014
SpecialSales@dk.com

Printed in China

A WORLD OF IDEAS:
SEE ALL THERE IS TO KNOW

www.starwars.com
www.dk.com

Contents

Into the stars

The galaxy is a big place, with millions of planets in it—and it is yours to explore. But you are going to need a ride! Maybe you will take a spin in a speedy starfighter. Perhaps cruising in a silver starship is more your style. With luck, you will steer clear of the terrifying Super Star Destroyers!

In the huge galaxy you need space vehicles for getting around. There are thousands of different ships zooming among the stars. Some carry just one passenger, while others move an entire army. This book shows you all the coolest and most important spacecraft.

Welcome to the galaxy. Step in, buckle up, and enjoy the ride!

WELCOME TO NABOO

Theed

Naboo's capital city is known for its incredible architecture. The stunning Royal Palace built on the edge of a sheer cliff is a must-see sight for any visitor.

Lake retreat

Surrounded by mountains and stunning waterfalls, this location is the perfect place for a romantic getaway or a secret wedding.

Otoh Gunga

Located underwater, this lovely city is made using unique Gungan technology. The shapes and lights make the city glisten like a jewel.

Great Grass Plains

Located to the south of the city of Theed is an area named the Great Grass Plains. Dramatic battles have taken place here but its beauty is better suited to relaxing hikes.

Droid Control Ship

The Trade Federation is a powerful group of greedy merchants from all over the galaxy. Its leaders fly around in large, donut-shaped cargo ships.

The Trade Federation is unhappy with the Galactic Republic, which rules the galaxy. To prepare for war, the Trade Federation secretly changes its cargo ships into battleships.

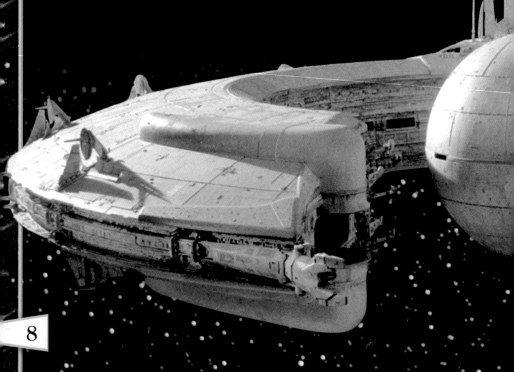

The battleships can carry weapons and robot soldiers called battle droids.

The Droid Control Ship is the most important ship in the Trade Federation's fleet of battleships. It contains computers and special equipment that operate the battle droids by remote control. The droids will not work without signals from the Control Ship.

The Trade Federation's leaders decide to show the Galactic Republic that they are powerful. So they attack the peaceful planet of Naboo.

Above Naboo, pilots control the Droid Control Ship from the ball-shaped Core Ship, which sits inside the outer ring. The Core Ship also contains the ship's reactor engine, but it is not well protected. A talented young pilot, Anakin Skywalker, discovers this for himself when he sets off a chain of explosions that destroys the Droid Control Ship. In Anakin's own words, "Oops!"

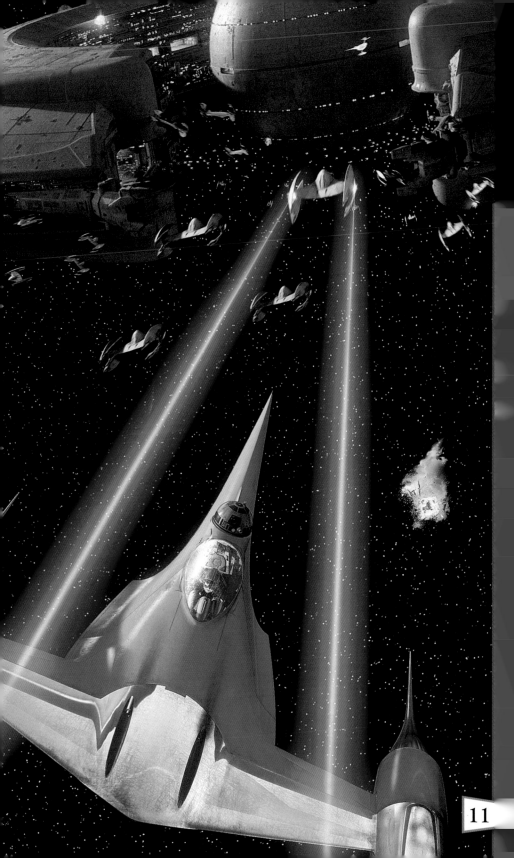

11

PAWNS OF

Darth Sidious has a secret plan to gain total control of the galaxy. To get what he wants he must hide his true identity and get others to do his dirty work.

TRADE FEDERATION

The Neimoidian leaders of the Trade Federation live in fear of Darth Sidious. They will do whatever he says.

DARTH SIDIOUS

The evil Sith Lord promises the greedy Trade Federation money and power if they accept his control.

THE SITH

SECRET ARMY

Following Darth Sidious's orders, the Trade Federation secretly creates a powerful droid army.

INVASION OF NABOO

The droid army is deployed on the planet Naboo, causing a galactic crisis.

Naboo Royal Starship

Inside and out, the Naboo Royal Starship is fit for a queen. Its engines and equipment are the very best. Inside, it is as beautiful as any palace. Everything is neat and tidy, right down to the ship's wires and cables. The starship is covered in shiny silver metal, a color only the queen's transport is allowed.

Because the Royal Starship travels on missions of peace, it is not armed with weapons. During her time as elected ruler of Naboo, Queen Amidala uses the Royal Starship to make official visits. Her bodyguards, loyal handmaidens, and the ship's crew always go with her.

Podracers

Gentlemen… and scoundrels!
Start your engines! Podracing is a
popular extreme sport in the galaxy.
Several dozen podracers race at a time,
ducking and diving through the course
at speeds of more than 500 miles
(800 kilometers) an hour. Pilots use
every skill they have to avoid crashing.

On the day of a big podrace, you can almost taste the excitement in the air. Or is that the smell of the strong fuel that powers these super-fast vehicles?

A basic podracer machine is made up of a cockpit, or control pod, where the pilot sits, attached by cables to a pair of engines. But no two podracers are alike!

Podracer pilots add extra bits of
machinery to their vehicles to make
them faster and so shave seconds
off their race times. Anakin Skywalker
is the only human good enough to
race. This nine-year-old boy is a skilled
mechanic. He improves his podracer,
which he built himself, with spare
parts he finds in the junk shop
where he works.

Anakin's mechanical skills are matched by his amazing performances as a pilot. Podracing fans are still talking about his victory in the famous Boonta Eve Classic Race, in which he beat the race favorite, Sebulba.

PODRACING STARS

Get ready for Tatooine's Boonta Eve Classic race—the greatest podracing spectacle this side of the galaxy! Let's meet some of the daring racers who are taking part today.

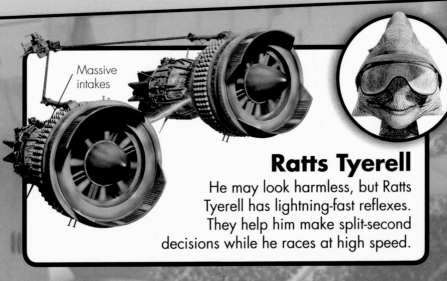

Massive intakes

Ratts Tyerell

He may look harmless, but Ratts Tyerell has lightning-fast reflexes. They help him make split-second decisions while he races at high speed.

Gasgano

Gasgano has 24 fingers. He can perform multiple tasks while racing, such as checking the oil, engine, and power.

Anti-turbulence vanes

Ben Quadinaros

Ben is an inexperienced podracer, who is more used to racing on the amateur circuit. Ben has rented a BT310 quadra-podracer specially to compete in the Boonta Eve Classic.

Fuel tank

Teemto Pagalies

Teemto discovered his talent for podracing after running away from home. He is very proud of his powerful IPG-X1131 Longtail podracer.

Energy-binder plate

Naboo N-1 starfighters

In times of peace, N-1 starfighter ships fly alongside the Queen of Naboo's Royal Starship. But in times of war, they may have to use their twin blaster cannons to get out of danger!

Once, Anakin Skywalker hides in an N-1 starfighter. He accidentally turns the engines on. The starfighter shoots into the air and flies into a fierce battle between the Trade Federation and Naboo. Anakin dodges heavy fire from the enemy ships. Using all the skills he learned as a podracer, he enters the Droid Control Ship and destroys its engines. Since the Trade Federation's army is controlled by the ship, Anakin ends the war and becomes a hero.

Slave I

When Jango Fett is after you in his starship *Slave I* there's nowhere to hide. Jango is a bounty hunter. He captures people who are on the run from the law and collects the reward for those he finds and delivers.

A good bounty hunter needs a ship that can go anywhere in the galaxy. The ship must be full of powerful weapons to use on anything in its way. It should also have a secure place to hold captives once they have been caught.

Jango stole *Slave I* from a prison so it already had on-board prison cells, but he made lots of improvements.

The main changes Jango made were
to the ship's weapons. It already had
blaster cannons, but he added lots
of extra hidden weaponry, including
laser cannons and torpedoes. He also
refitted the crew quarters inside the
ship to make even the longest
journeys possible. The prison cells
were changed to coffinlike
wall cabinets to make them
impossible to break out of.
Jango Fett often travels
with his son, Boba. Jango
pilots the ship, while young Boba
watches and learns from his father.
Later, when Boba Fett becomes
the owner of Slave I, he adds even
more powerful weapons to the ship.

HOW DO YOU OUTWIT A
BOUNTY HUNTER?

Ruthless bounty hunter Jango Fett is after Obi-Wan Kenobi. Usually there is no escape for Fett's victims. Obi-Wan must think fast to come up with a plan if he wants to survive.

1

ENEMY CLOSING IN

Increase ship's speed to try to outrun the bounty hunter's starfighter.

2

TAKE EVASIVE ACTION

Utilize expert flying maneuvers to avoid laser fire from the enemy starfighter.

3

THINK QUICKLY
If you're in an asteroid belt, try not to get hit by dangerous asteroids zipping by.

4

CREATE A DISTRACTION
Use exploding asteroids to make the bounty hunter think your ship has exploded.

5

STAY HIDDEN
Find a good hiding spot behind a large asteroid and wait for the bounty hunter to leave.

Republic gunships

When the Republic's defenders, the Jedi Knights, are surrounded by Trade Federation forces on the planet of Geonosis, the Republic gunships come to the rescue. These ships are a key part of any successful attack by the Republic. They can move army troops right into position, then take off at speed.

Each Republic gunship can transport a team of 30 soldiers and 4 speeder bikes to hot spots on the battlefield. Its thick hull resists enemy fire. It can fly through heavy cannon fire and escape with only a few dents. The Republic gunships can also swoop down to attack ground troops and land vehicles.

Jedi starfighters

In the heat of a star battle, every second counts. Jedi Knights like Anakin Skywalker and Obi-Wan Kenobi count on their starships to help them slip through a war zone unharmed. They often fly into battle alongside larger ships like the ARC-170.

Anakin is training to be a Jedi. His starfighter is small but powerful. It was once a standard Jedi starship, but Anakin uses his skills as a mechanic to improve the vessel. He removed heavy flight instruments and bulky shields for greater speed and control. He even changed its color to yellow to remind him of his old podracer.

Invisible Hand

The Trade Federation's flagship, *Invisible Hand*, is the most advanced starship in the fleet. Its shields and super-thick hull help to protect it from attack by enemy ships.

In one incredible battle, the leader of the Republic, Chancellor Palpatine, is captured and held prisoner on the ship.

Obi-Wan Kenobi and Anakin rush to rescue the Chancellor from the Trade Federation. Inside the *Invisible Hand*, the Jedi defeat Chancellor Palpatine's captors, but the ship catches fire. Even though it breaks in half, Anakin manages to land what's left of the vessel before it is destroyed by flames.

Escape pods

There are times when a quick getaway is best, especially when lives are in danger. For those times, an escape pod is a very welcome sight.

Most large starships, and even some planets, have escape pods. Smaller ships, such as starfighters, have ejector seats. These ejector seats throw the pilot out of a damaged ship to safety.

Escape pods are like lifeboats. Some are only big enough for one person. Others are designed to hold many people.

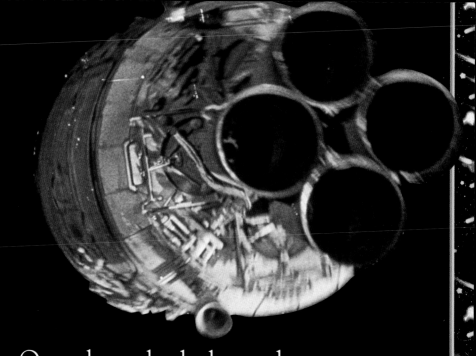

Once launched, the pods automatically find the nearest planet to land on. A typical escape pod has enough supplies to keep the occupants safe and alive until they are rescued.

Every escape pod is fitted with communications equipment. This means that the passengers can send out calls for help. They just have to hope that their messages are received by someone friendly!

Imperial shuttles

The peaceful Republic has been taken over by Palpatine. He is really an evil schemer, whose only goal is power. The Republic is now Palpatine's Empire, and he has made himself Emperor.

Palpatine uses an Imperial shuttle as his personal transport. The sight of the Emperor's ship arriving like a giant bird of prey strikes fear into all who hate the Empire. Important Imperial officers also use these shuttles to get around.

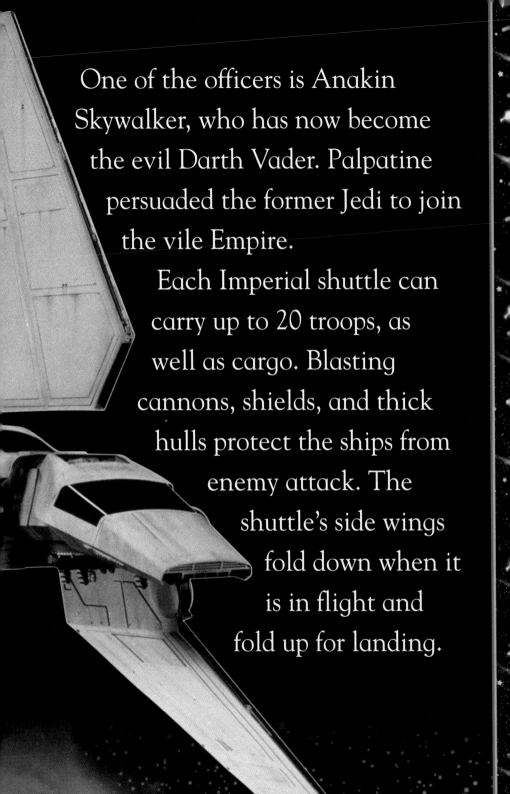

One of the officers is Anakin
Skywalker, who has now become
the evil Darth Vader. Palpatine
persuaded the former Jedi to join
the vile Empire.
Each Imperial shuttle can
carry up to 20 troops, as
well as cargo. Blasting
cannons, shields, and thick
hulls protect the ships from
enemy attack. The
shuttle's side wings
fold down when it
is in flight and
fold up for landing.

TIE fighters

The small ships called TIE fighters are the main starfighters of the Imperial forces. The ships are simple and cheap to build because they are made in vast numbers. TIE stands for the Twin Ion Engines that power these small ships. TIE fighters attack one after another, sometimes hundreds at a time.

A single TIE fighter may be easy to destroy, but for each one shot down, a thousand more appear. To make these fighters go faster there is no heavy equipment on the ships. The only weapons are two laser cannons. Often, dozens of TIE fighters fire their cannons at the same time to greatly increase their power.

Piloting a TIE fighter is a risky business. There is no life-support system on board so the pilots must wear a protective suit.

The ships are speedy and move around quickly, but they have no special shields to protect them from enemy fire. The fighters are easy targets from the side because of their large wings. It's a good thing there seems to be a steady supply of TIE pilots! TIE fighters have been involved in many fierce battles with enemies of the Empire, including the freedom fighters of the Rebel Alliance.

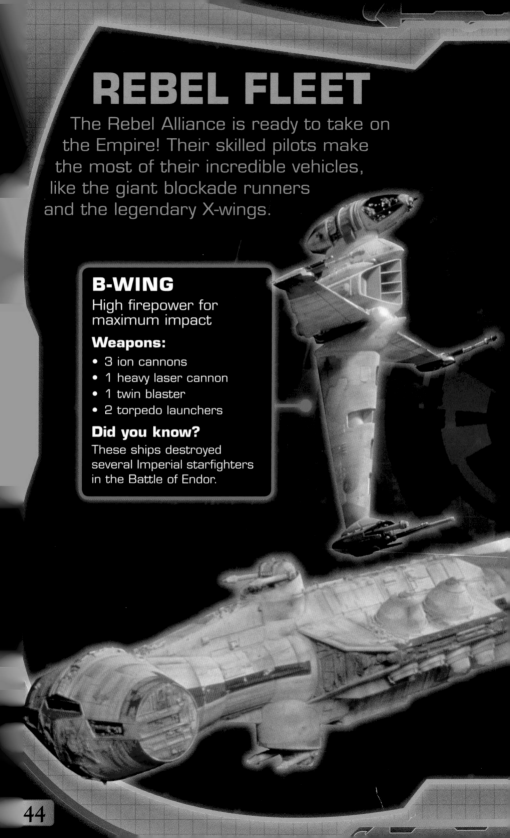

REBEL FLEET

The Rebel Alliance is ready to take on the Empire! Their skilled pilots make the most of their incredible vehicles, like the giant blockade runners and the legendary X-wings.

B-WING

High firepower for maximum impact

Weapons:

- 3 ion cannons
- 1 heavy laser cannon
- 1 twin blaster
- 2 torpedo launchers

Did you know?

These ships destroyed several Imperial starfighters in the Battle of Endor.

X-WING

Perfect balance of
speed and firepower

Weapons:
- 4 laser cannons
- 12 torpedo launchers

Did you know?
The X-wing is famous
for destroying the first
Death Star.

A-WING

High speed ideal for
quick attacks

Weapons:
- 2 laser cannons
- 2 missile launchers

Did you know?
An A-wing once successfully
blew up a Super Star Destroyer.

REBEL BLOCKADE RUNNER

Powerful engine can outrun almost anything

Weapons:
- 2 double turbolaser turrets
- 4 single turbolaser turrets

Did you know?
A blockade runner served as Princess Leia's
personal transport ship.

Millennium Falcon

You wouldn't know it from its battered outside, but the *Millennium Falcon* is one of the fastest vessels in the galaxy. It is owned by Han Solo, a one-time smuggler who fights with the Rebel Alliance against the Empire.

The saucer-shaped craft gets its super-speed from its hyperdrive engine, which Han has adjusted to make it go even faster. The starship also carries a variety of powerful equipment, such as top-of-the-line sensors, quad-laser cannons, and missile launchers.

The *Millennium Falcon*'s hull is beaten, battle-scarred, and looks ready for the repair shop. But Han and his copilot, the Wookiee Chewbacca, have made many improvements to their starship. They added hidden blaster cannons, escape pods, and secret compartments.

Now, it is even capable of outrunning an Imperial TIE fighter! These modifications make the *Millennium Falcon* perfect for rescue missions. In fact, Han, Chewbacca, Luke Skywalker, and Obi-Wan Kenobi used the *Falcon* to rescue rebel leader Princess Leia from the Empire.

INSIDE THE
MILLENNIUM FALCON

Concealed blaster cannon

Han Solo in the pilot's seat

Maintenance bay

Sensor antenna

Landing jet

Main hold

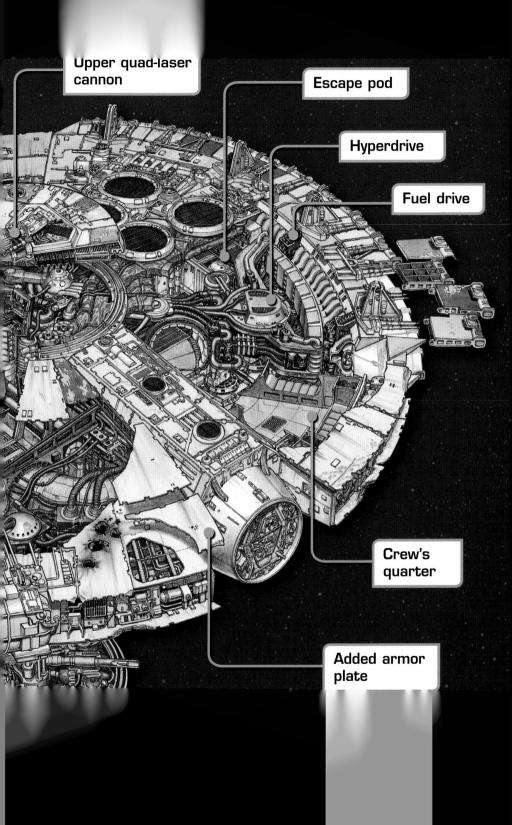

Upper quad-laser cannon

Escape pod

Hyperdrive

Fuel drive

Crew's quarter

Added armor plate

X-wing starfighters

An X-wing starfighter is the little ship that destroys the Empire's first Death Star, a huge super-weapon. Of course, Luke Skywalker, the brave young Rebel Alliance pilot at the controls that day, has Jedi powers to guide him.

But his choice of starship definitely
helps him beat the odds.

The X-wings get their name from
the shape of their wings. In battle,
the wings split into an X-shape.
At the end of each wing is a
powerful laser cannon.

The X-wings are the starfighters
of the Rebel Alliance. These speedy
starships are equipped with torpedo
launchers and have special equipment
to help guide the pilot.

The Rebel Alliance works out a
plan to destroy the Death Star. If the
deadly super-weapon's engine can be
hit by a torpedo, it will explode.

To do this, a pilot must land a torpedo into a small hole in a deep, dark trench. Many rebels try, but it is only future Jedi Luke Skywalker, with a little help from Han Solo in the *Millennium Falcon*, who hits the target.

The Death Star is blown to pieces! The X-wing becomes a legend among Rebel Alliance pilots.

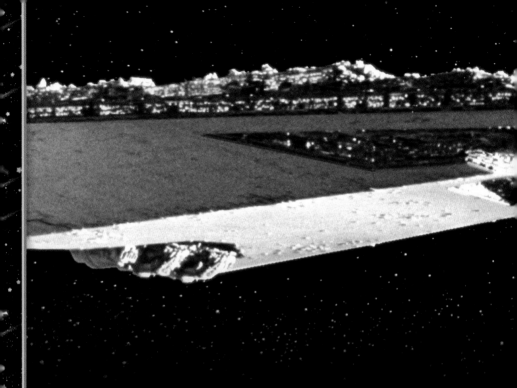

Super Star Destroyer

Many things come in large sizes. Some things come in extra-large sizes. But the Super Star Destroyer *Executor* is so big, it is almost off the scale! It is the largest starship in the galaxy, at an incredible 11.8 miles (19,000 meters) long. This terrifying dagger-shaped giant is evil Darth Vader's command ship.

The Super Star Destroyer's enormous
size is a symbol of the strength and
power of the Empire.

Darth Vader's starship is stocked
with more than 1,000 deadly weapons,
ready to use in any attack on the Rebel
Alliance. It can also carry thousands
of troops, starfighters, vehicles, and
other military equipment.

The Super Star Destroyer's deflector-shield dome helps protect the ship from attack, and the communications tower makes sure the ship gets its messages across loud and clear. The *Executor* is the first of many Super Star Destroyers to be built by the Empire with the aim of crushing all of its enemies.

But even these ships cannot stop the Rebel Alliance. During one battle, an out-of-control Rebel Alliance A-wing starfighter crashes into the *Executor's* bridge. The blast damages the Super Star Destroyer's controls. The giant ship can no longer resist the pull of the second Death Star, and the two collide in a spectacular explosion.

Glossary

Empire
A group of nations ruled over by one leader, who is called an Emperor.

Federation
A group of countries or organizations that work together because they have the same aims.

Hyperdrive
A device that makes starships travel at incredibly high speeds.

Imperial
Something from or belonging to the Empire.

Jedi Knight
A warrior with special powers who defends the galaxy from evil.

Republic
A nation or group of nations in which the people vote for their leaders.

Smuggler
Someone who transports things secretly to make money from selling them.

Index

Guide for Parents

DK Readers is a four-level interactive reading adventure series for children, developing the habit of reading widely for both pleasure and information. These books have an exciting main narrative interspersed with a range of reading genres to suit your child's reading ability, as required by the Common Core State Standards. Each book is designed to develop your child's reading skills, fluency, grammar awareness, and comprehension in order to build confidence and engagement when reading.

Ready for a *Reading Alone* book
YOUR CHILD SHOULD

- be able to read most words without needing to stop and break them down into sound parts.
- read smoothly, in phrases and with expression. By this level, your child will be mostly reading silently.
- self-correct when some word or sentence doesn't sound right.

A Valuable and Shared Reading Experience

For some children, text reading, particularly nonfiction, requires much effort, but adult participation can make this both fun and easier. So here are a few tips on how to use this book with your child.

TIP 1 Check out the contents together before your child begins:

- Invite your child to check the blurb, contents page, and layout of the book and comment on it.
- Ask your child to make predictions about the story.
- Talk about the information your child might want to find out.

TIP 2 Encourage fluent and flexible reading:

- Support your child to read in fluent, expressive phrases, making full use of punctuation and thinking about the meaning.

- Encourage your child to slow down and check information where appropriate.

TIP 3 Indicators that your child is reading for meaning:

- Your child will be responding to the text if he/she is self-correcting and varying his/her voice.
- Your child will want to talk about what he/she is reading or is eager to turn the page to find out what will happen next.

TIP 4 Share and discuss:

- Encourage your child to recall specific details after each chapter.
- Provide opportunities for your child to pick out interesting words and discuss what they mean.
- Discuss how the author captures the reader's interest, or how effective the nonfiction layouts are.
- Ask questions about the text. These help develop comprehension skills and awareness of the language used.

A FEW ADDITIONAL TIPS

- Read to your child regularly to demonstrate fluency, phrasing, and expression; to find out or check information; and for sharing enjoyment.
- Encourage your child to reread favorite texts to increase reading confidence and fluency.
- Check that your child is reading a range of different types of material, such as poems, jokes, and following instructions.

- Series consultant, **Dr. Linda Gambrell**, Distinguished Professor of Education at Clemson University, has served as President of the National Reading Conference, the College Reading Association, and the International Reading Association. She is also reading consultant for the **DK Adventures.**

Have you read these other great books from DK?

READING ALONE ③

Test what makes rockets fly. Which design would you use?

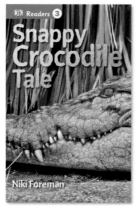

Follow Chris Croc's adventures from a baby to king of the river.

Join the heroes of the rebellion as they continue to fight the Empire.

Learn all about Yoda's battles and how he uses the Force.

Can Luke Skywalker help the rebels defeat the evil Empire?

Meet the heroes of Chima™ and help them find the Legend Beasts.